William Lloyd Garrison, engraving from 1879

THE PHILOSOPHER ABOLITIONIST: WILLIAM L. GARRISON'S LIFE IN IDEAS

By

Timothy Pifer

Copyright © 2015 Timothy Pifer

All rights reserved.

ISBN: 1515244083
ISBN-13: 978-1515244080

DEDICATION

To Nancy.

Cover page image: William Lloyd Garrison, engraving from 1879 (File:WilliamLloydGarrison.JPG-(Public Domain) from Wikimedia Commons)

CONTENTS

Contents	i
Acknowledgments	iii
1. Introduction	1
2. Research Methodology and The Garrison Collection	4
3. Garrison's Life	7
4. Childhood	10
5. Apprenticeship	18
6. Conversion to Abolition	24
7. Professional Abolitionist	28
8. Ideological Battles	34
9. Garrisonians and Non-Garrisonians	47
10. Popular Prophet and the Republican Advocate	54
11. Post War Retirement	58
12. Historiographical Review	61
13. Conclusion	68
Selected Bibliography	72
About the Author	76
Endnotes	77

Timothy Pifer

ACKNOWLEDGMENTS

Special thanks to my wife, Nancy. She has proven time after time to be a proofreader extraordinaire and the source of my best ideas. Also, I want to thank the University of Louisville History Department's faculty and staff that encouraged my history studies and gave me the confidence to write this book on William Lloyd Garrison.

1 INTRODUCTION

The objective of this book is to provide a biographical and historiographical examination of the noted abolitionist leader, William Lloyd Garrison. Garrison is well worth studying since he was uniquely positioned at the heart of the Immediate Abolitionist movement which advocated no delay in granting freedom to slaves as opposed to gradual emancipation. Garrison (1805-1879) was perhaps the best-known and most radical immediate abolitionist of the Antebellum period, and was closely associated at various times with other notables such as Wendell Phillips, Harriet Beecher Stowe, and Frederick Douglass. Some historians have even described his role as being uniquely indispensable to the early days of abolitionism, viewing him as the movement's spiritual leader and the center of philosophical discord within the movement's hierarchy. In fact, the key philosophical differences within the movement have even been characterized by academic journals as divisions between Garrisonian and anti-Garrisonian factions. Noted historian Aileen S. Kraditor goes so far as to say, "… the personal and ideological idiosyncrasies of William Lloyd Garrison have been used to set the tone for discussions of the whole movement."[1]   No study of the Antebellum period is complete without a study of Garrison's life and personal philosophy.

Another intent of this book is to try and account for the wildly differing interpretations of Garrison's motivations and principles both by his contemporaries and subsequent historians. Throughout his life Garrison was an idealistic man who defined himself and others in the framework of his individual morality and philosophy. Therefore, any biography must also study the evolution of Garrison's personal ideology to understand its outward effect on others. As previously noted, Garrison's public expression of ideas often provoked controversy and differences of opinion. So perhaps it is understandable that there are as many different opinions about the wily abolitionist as there are authors writing about him. In other words, Garrison is perfect fodder for further research and debate.

2 RESEARCH METHODOLOGY AND THE GARRISON COLLECTION

The methodology to explore Garrison's life and later academic works about his time on earth was an analysis of both primary and secondary sources. Research for this book was founded on observations by his contemporaries, period publications such as the newspaper the *Liberator*, and related published observations in journals and books by later historians. In the absence of an actual autobiography a six volume set of Garrison's correspondence running almost the entirety of his life has been used here to arrive at his own reflections about his life and controversial ideas.[2]

Originally, various scholars had collected the letters until finally historians Walter Merrill and Louis Ruchames assembled and edited them into a multi-volume set with publication occurring from 1971 to 1981. The six volumes span Garrison's life from 1822 until his death in 1879. In all, the six volumes contain 1,527 separate pieces of correspondence which were presented in a chronological sequence. The first four volumes contain all the known letters by Garrison that were available at the time of the volumes' publication. The correspondence presented consisted of private letters to family, friends and associates as well as public letters to editors of publications and civic leaders.[3] The four volumes run from Garrison's first letter to the editor of the *Newburyport Herald* on May 21, 1822[4] until his December 1, 1861 letter to James Redpath attacking the institution of slavery.[5] The last two volumes of the series encompass only a select percentage of the available items and were mostly drawn from Garrison's public letters (Volume five contains forty percent of his letters from 1861 to 1867[6] while Volume six contains twenty percent from 1868 until 1879[7]).

Garrison never appeared reluctant to discuss any topic or idea in his many personal and public letters. He was willing to discuss his rather unorthodox confidence in spiritualism and mediums saying such things as, "I am a firm believer in the reality of those Manifestations"[8] and "The best medium I have ever seen is a Mrs. Tribou ... She is most reliable, and remarkable as a writing, rapping, tipping, healing, and personating medium."[9] He even detailed the deadly scalding of his son Charles during a medical treatment at home, "Alas! on coming out of the bath, we found that the poor boy had been horribly scalded ... from that fatal hour he became delirious ...."[10] Given the uninhibited nature of Garrison's correspondence it is reasonable to conclude that if he held a strong belief or position it would emerge somewhere in his voluminous writings. It is expected that an examination of Garrison's letters along with other sources of research will reveal his fundamental values and allow insight into his personal philosophy.

3 GARRISON'S LIFE

The following is an examination of Garrison's life as seen through his ideology. The reason for this approach was that Garrison saw the world through his own unique intellectual filter and rarely took counsel from the prevailing cultural views. Furthermore, ideas and communicating them became his stock and trade as he found his way in the greater world. As a public speaker, writer, paper editor, publisher, and social advocate, Garrison's professional life was always an expression of his individual philosophy and idiosyncratically based ideas. Additionally, his personal life experiences were also shaped directly by his belief structure. His response to his family and his network of friends was built fundamentally upon his ideology. His friendships and social relationships with groups and institutions were dramatically affected by his particular beliefs at any given time. Ultimately, his interaction with the world was controlled and shaped by his personal ideology.

As will be seen, Garrison's ideology was not a fixed structure unaltered by his transition through life. Rather his personal ideology changed and evolved. Admittedly there were some fundamental beliefs that held true throughout such as his dislike of slavery and alcohol, and the need for social reform in the United States. But even his fundamental ideology on core issues transformed and mutated over time. He also showed the ability to adapt his ideas not only to changes in his own life but also the greater events shaping his culture and nation. Therefore, his existence and ideological belief structure were completely interrelated making the study of one almost indistinguishable from the other. In other words, Garrison's ideas and beliefs make an excellent guidepost for structuring a biography of his life beginning with his early life straight through to the end.

4 CHILDHOOD

The son of an often out of work merchant sailor, William Lloyd Garrison was born on December 12, 1805 in the small town of Newburyport, Massachusetts. He was the next to the youngest child of four with an older brother James and a sister Caroline who died when she was just five years of age, and younger sister Maria.[11] Garrison's personal understanding of the need for social improvements in the Antebellum period manifested during this time. He grew up in rather humble surroundings in a lower class family. His early view of society was in fact seen from the bottom rungs as a genuinely underprivileged child.[12] The need for social reform and other fundamental beliefs therefore traced back to this early New England childhood and upbringing.

From both his parents he would develop important aspects of his ideology. His father Abijah Garrison led the family into financial failure. This loss of social standing was due in no small part to the bad economic times in New England seaports and a Jeffersonian foreign policy that included a crippling embargo on trade with Europe. As a result, Abijah spent most of his days and money in the grog houses until he walked out on the family and forever out of young William's life.[13] This placed the responsibility for three small children solely on his mother Maria. Maria was an extremely religious person who tried to instill in her children her own deep religious beliefs. These beliefs would take hold in William and his sister but his brother would follow his father to the sea joining the navy and becoming a lifelong alcoholic. Through her revivalist-styled Baptist church Sister Garrison as she was called found menial jobs and maintained a precarious life of poverty. As result of this harsh life William's mother would die a broken woman when he was just beginning his newspaper career.[14]

From these early beginnings Garrison began to work out some of the ideas that would shape him for the remainder of his life. From his alcoholic absentee father Garrison drew an object lesson on the seamier aspects of life. In addition to the obvious connection to his professional temperance leanings, there were also connections to his personal life. For example, in spite of his many professional obligations throughout his long life Garrison was a devoted father and caring family man. Garrison always believed that he was responsible for the welfare of his family and providing a fine middle class life style.[15] In a letter to his wife during their courtship, he relates that he is motivated by his duty to humanity and not because of money though he does not spurn 'earthly comforts',

> Engaged in the noblest cause of benevolence which has ever received the approbation of God, or the countenance of man, I am necessarily precluded from heaping up treasures upon earth. But little do I covet those treasures . . . But I shall not lack a full supply of earthly comforts. – All the aid that I shall need, will be liberally extended to me. If my enemies are bitter and numerous, my friends are proportionally kind and steadfast. The prospect is truly encouraging.[16]

By means of his benefactors and his own efforts, Garrison was able to maintain a comfortable household for a large family. He even was able to regularly employ maids, "Girl after girl has come, and proved inexperienced or worthless – how many, I will not begin to enumerate . . . . With our large family, to be without someone to do the cooking and washing, even for twenty-four hours, is a serious inconvenience."[17]

From his mother, Garrison would receive a deep belief in the power of religion. The deep spiritual convictions of Frances Maria Garrison would be reflected in most of his writings and his speeches later in life. As an adult Garrison stated his private feelings to a friend on religion and the sanctity of the Bible, "my religious views are of the most elevated, the most spiritual character; that I esteem the holy scriptures above all books in the universe . . . ."[18] In fact, his fundamental public arguments against slavery would include a truly religious bent. He explained the need for immediate emancipation was because slavery was a sin against God requiring an undeviating end to the holy transgression.[19] Throughout his life Garrison rarely wrote or spoke without invoking God or the Bible.

Perhaps he also drew upon his mother for some of his ideas on devotion to one's family. In an 1834 letter to his wife Garrison spoke of his late mother's devotion, "I had another once, who cared for me with such a passionate regard, who loved me so intensely, that no language can describe the yearnings of her soul."[20] He spoke in similar words about his own family and his devotion, "not that I am forgetful of the sacred claims which are binding upon me as a husband and a father."[21] His mother was a stark reflection of the sacrifice Garrison saw of a parent to one's family which he internalized in his correspondence, ideology, and the treatment of his children. John L. Thomas discussed in his book *The Liberator* that Garrison developed from his strong willed mother a lasting respect for other strong women that manifested in his support of the women's right movement.[22]

Finally, his need to join the middle class and his less than total support and sympathy to the plight of the working class can perhaps in some way link to his childhood. His repeated assertions that he was a great businessman even when money was difficult may have been caused by his earliest recollections. Garrison received much of his financial support for the *Liberator* through donations from white abolition philanthropists and contributions from freed black communities. Nevertheless, he apparently always believed that he was a very successful independent businessman and entrepreneur. In fact, his explanation for the donations make it seem like they were part of his business model, "Every year, donations to a considerable amount were required to keep the paper in existence; but this pecuniary burden was borne with great cheerfulness by a few personal friends, because they believed that they could not devote their money to a better purpose, and the downfall of the *Liberator* would prove serious injury to the anti-slavery enterprise."[23] There are numerous other examples in the correspondence where Garrison offered himself self-congratulations on his business skills and money management. In an 1835 letter Garrison talks about how other, better supported, papers had failed, "How many religious and political papers have perished, (though supported by sectarian and political zeal,) since we started the *Liberator*, a paper of an Ishmaeltish character!"[24] In addition, there were his comments about the idea of the 1867 testimonial fund being placed in a trust to be managed by others, "I am particularly sensitive on this point, because whatever failings I may have, the misuse of money has never been one of them."[25] This outlook about his career and financial gain is one that Garrison maintains throughout his life.

In his letters Garrison seemed most desirous of his middle class standing and rejected the farmer and worker class. In one letter he comments to his wife that, "A country life is exceedingly monotonous, presenting no other phase than that of habitual stillness and uniformity."[26] Garrison never gave the impression that he believed he, his family, or the nation should forsake the middle class life and return to the 'good old days' of agrarian based economics. Nor was he one to view the problems of workers as other than ones that must be dealt with just as he had raised himself from poverty to respectable businessman. In an 1875 letter Garrison summed up his feelings on the subject of the oppressed working class,

> I cannot feel any heartrending emotions, therefore, or give vent to any special indignation, in contemplating the condition of people who are not under despotic or dynastic sway . . . with the rights conscience, who enjoy the right to assemble, whenever or wherever they please, to seek redress for real and imaginary grievances, who are free to make their own contracts and sell or employ their labor according to the law of supply and demand . . .[27]

It is from his early life that one can see the ideas and events that shape a young Garrison. His concern about the problems society inflicted upon the less fortunate was seen from the viewpoint of an adolescent victim. His humble beginnings also provoked strong religious beliefs that found their way into his antislavery ideals. In the absence of wealth and the material elements of life Garrison was naturally drawn to more cerebral pursuits to escape his impoverishment. But this was just the beginning of Garrison's ideological journey in his lifetime.

5 APPRENTICESHIP

With his childhood experiences Garrison had developed a basic ideology to understand his world. The next phase of his life was the development of the skills to use and communicate his ideas to others. Because of their financial difficulties young Garrison did not have the opportunity of much schooling. Rather than an academic education his mother began him in various apprentice programs such as shoe making and cabinet making. However, it was not until he began an apprenticeship to a newspaper editor that Garrison showed any real abilities and interest.

He served first under a Mr. Allen the editor of the *Newburyport Herald* as a typesetter, a hands-on job he would enjoy the rest of his life. In addition, Garrison tried his hand commenting in a series of letters to the paper. He wrote under the name "Old Bachelor's"[28] on subjects as varied as love, fortune hunting and adventures at sea. He even discussed the issue of slavery in one of his public letters saying that it was not a threat to the nation but that little virtue "exist in the morals of a people among whom slaves abound."[29] Ironically his loving mother tried to talk him out of writing as a career for fear he could not earn a living. Still, he was not discouraged and in an 1823 letter wrote with great pride of his published letters, "since I commenced writing for the Herald. . . . I have met with signal success. . . ."[30] He found time away from the newspaper to join a local debate club and began practicing his public speaking skills.[31] In addition to beginning his newspaper and public speaking career Garrison was also developing new ideas and refining earlier ones.

In particular, Garrison took the role of Federalist advocate as demonstrated by his public attack on General Jackson's run for the White House, "your fellow countrymen, perceive your unfitness for office to which you and so many are aspiring."[32] He was also an advocate for other causes. He was against a 1827 tariff proposal in Congress citing in an open letter to the *Boston Courier* "I will state that my feelings are equally strong with his, in favor of commerce and against an exorbitant tariff"[33] and on another occasion, "I am satisfied that the true source of national wealth arises preeminently not from the encouragement of any branch of industry, but from a fair and liberal support to all."[34] Interestingly, the socially radical Garrison was to become a pro-business idealist his entire life. Even after becoming active in the Immediate Abolitionist movement he said in the *Liberator*, "We shall be able, ere long, to supply not only our home consumption, but the wants of the Southern Republics … and here opens a new world of wealth to be gathered by our merchants and manufacturers."[35], and "… the protection of American industry is the life-blood of the nation."[36] However, at this time Garrison still lacked a unifying ideology to focus his advocate efforts once he struck out on his own.

As young new editor Garrison would try three different newspapers in the late 1820s before making his fateful move to Baltimore. On each occasion Garrison failed to find the winning combination for a successful paper. It was a combination of bad luck and not finding the right message for the customers of each paper. Garrison had the idea that he wanted to become a social commentator on the various ills of the culture. In his first newspaper, the Federalist-oriented Newburyport *Free Press,* he made light of some local political dirty tricks and caused a backlash of bad press by his new found political enemies that cost him his editorship.[37] This inauspicious first foray into the political arena would be a harbinger for his rejection of the Liberty and Free Soil Parties. His next attempt at editorship was in Boston with the temperance centered *National Philanthropist*, which incorporated witty verses such as, "What is the cause of every ill? That does with pain the body fill? It is the repeated gill Of Whiskey."[38] Here Garrison served his six months contract and left the newspaper under rumors that he wasn't offered another contract. Returning to Newburyport Garrison tried again with the *Journal of the Times* another pro-Federalist paper. Here Garrison expands his ideas into other areas to include gradual emancipation as advocated by the American Colonization Society (ACS). But he is again going up against an established paper where he had apprenticed under Mr. Allen and was unable to steal away needed readers before closing shop.[39] In all these newspapers Garrison had not found his readership or his true message. But in Boston he met a man who would help him find his ideological calling and his professional purpose in life.

In 1828 while serving on the *National Philanthropist* he met a middle-aged Quaker printer visiting Boston named Benjamin Lundy. Lundy published a paper called the *Genius of Universal Emancipation* that sparked young Garrison's attention. Amidst the attempts to start his own newspaper in 1828 Garrison conversed with Lundy on the subject of slavery. The interest was mutual because Lundy walked from Baltimore to Boston in 1829 to persuade the young twenty-two year old editor to join his newspaper. Another indicator of Garrison's blossoming interest was his Boston speech to the city's Congregational societies and the ACS. He spoke for perhaps the first time in public on the issue of slavery at the Fourth of July ceremony to a group that, "bids fair to be overwhelming."[40] By September of the same year Garrison joins Lundy in Baltimore to publish a new version of the *Genius*.

6 CONVERSION TO ABOLITION

It was during this time working with Lundy that Garrison made his transition to an immediate end to slavery position, transforming into the abolitionist Garrison known to history. Different historians have attributed various reasons to Garrison for embracing the immediate abolitionist stance. For example, one idea is that his exposure to Blacks in Baltimore and particularly his reading of Black abolitionist David Walker's *Appeal* greatly influenced Garrison to convert from gradual to immediate emancipation.[41] Another suggested reason was that Garrison, like other White abolitionists, was driven into the immediate abolition movement because of failing in the new market economy.[42] Then again, the time he spent in jail for libeling Newburyport merchant Francis Todd (he had alleged that Todd had a business relationship with a notorious southern slave trader named Austin Woolfolk) has been put forth as providing Garrison with the time to reflect and develop his new ideas on slavery.[43] Garrison served time in jail until the New York abolitionist and wealthy philanthropist Arthur Tappan paid his hundred dollar fine forty-nine days later.[44] Another theory is that Garrison was a total convert to immediate abolitionism before leaving Boston and joining Lundy in Baltimore.[45] In this scenario Garrison was only humoring Lundy that he a devotee to the ACS and was just biding his time until he could strike out on his own. Still another basis given for Garrison becoming an immediate abolitionist was that he, like other leaders of the movement, "internalized the religious dictates of dominating mothers."[46] The possible causes of Garrison's break with Lundy and the ACS covers a wide spectrum of explanations and motivations. In the absence of clear and indisputable proof reasonable conjecture is that a combination of reasons resulted in Garrison's conversion.

    Regardless of all the discussion about the controlling factor which transformed Garrison into the archetypical immediate abolitionist, he really did change during this point in life into a public advocate for ending slavery now and not at some unknown time in the far future. He also demonstrated the talent to internalize his experiences and adapt his ideology to changing events. He would continue to display this talent throughout his life both professionally and personally. Moreover, Garrison was able to change his ideological stance from time to time without changing his core values. As a well known author on the abolitionist movement stated,

> Most of all I was increasingly struck by the logical consistency of his thought on all subjects. This is not to say his opinions did not change . . . . But the changes themselves represented a logical development, and I discovered no mutually invalidating convictions or torturing of logic . . . .[47]

His transition to the immediate abolitionist position seems to fit with his earlier ideas and experiences. He had been a young editor and burgeoning social advocate looking for a cause, and he had found one that appealed to his ideology.

7 PROFESSIONAL ABOLITIONIST

Garrison was now a professional advocate for the immediate end of slavery and prepared to expend all his professional energies towards that goal. It was the beginning of the 1830s that Garrison began his most productive time in the Immediate Abolitionist movement. His ideological assault on slavery took the form of a two prong attack beginning with his new newspaper, the *Liberator*. Unlike his earlier attempts the *Liberator*, in conjunction with his public speaking engagements, would serve as the very public voice of his personal ideas to the nation.

In fact, many people use the issue of the *Liberator* published on 1 January 1831 as the start date for the nation's entire Immediate

Abolitionist movement.[48] Garrison began without any financial assets, no actual subscribers and only his ideas as capital. He established intellectual holdings in the letterhead of the first issue that this was not to be just a local newspaper when he said, "Our Country is the World and our Countrymen are Mankind."[49] Moreover, he was confident that his ideas would be heeded when he stated, "I am earnest - I will not equivocate - I will not excuse - I will not retreat a single inch - and I WILL BE HEARD."[50] The *Liberator*, the longest continuously published abolitionist newspaper, served as the thirty plus year manifesto of Garrison and his followers' antislavery beliefs.

Through his innovative marketing ideas he turned the *Liberator* and other financial efforts into a combination of a political special interest group, national public advocacy organization, and a weekly publication containing news, articles, commentary and advertisements.[51] One article actually wrote on the subject of the *Liberator* and its innovative advertising of abolitionist labeled consumer goods. These good ran the gamut from abolitionist candy to books and the article called it, "the vanguard of capitalist liberalism."[52] By running the *Liberator* like a modern charity selling special interest items, publishing for a niche audience, and taking donations from wealthy benefactors Garrison was able to maintain a middle class lifestyle most of his adult life. He was able to lobby for his cause full time, raise and educate his large family, maintain a home, employ servants, travel abroad extensively, entertain visitors regularly, and retire comfortably.

Admittedly, he had precarious and continuous cash flow problems and equity difficulties almost all his career. Garrison was perpetually borrowing money, fund raising, running speaking tours, and selling subscriptions to the *Liberator*. He freely talked about his reoccurring money problems, ". . . I now stand in debt . . . unable to pay either my rent, or my grocer's bill, and my credit is, of course, suffering."[53] In spite of the financial problems that plagued the paper its entire thirty-four years in circulation and a readership that numbered only in the low thousands, the *Liberator* helped make Garrison a nationwide figure with his ideas reverberating in the national press and even finding its way into the lexicon of the Deep South. As a trained editor and publisher the newspaper provided Garrison a perfect outlet for his various ideas. Amazingly, he still was able to make a living just by selling his social reform ideas to the public through this and other forums.

The second prong of his attack was his critical participation in the formation of the Immediate Anti-Slavery Societies in the 1830s. This was an important objective as Garrison had, "a deep conviction that without the organization of abolitionists into societies, THE CAUSE WILL BE LOST."[54] Beginning in 1832, Garrison with a few followers founded the first New-England Anti-Slavery Society (NEASS). He dominated the first meetings and drafted the society's constitution to include the immediate abolitionist preamble, "immediate freedom from personal bondage of whatever kind, unless imposed by the sentence of law, for commission of some crime."[55] Even when an abolitionist Quaker named Arnold Buffum was elected president there was little doubt among the members present that it was Garrison's ideas that ruled the organization's ideology and tactics. Garrison seemed content with filling the role as the association's secretary and controlling the NEASS through his philosophical dictates. The first mission was to begin a series of petition campaigns directed at the United States Congress that would become popular among other abolitionist groups in the 1830s and 1840s. In fact, petitions became so popular that by 1840 the House of Representatives banned them from any legislative consideration. Another early mission of the organization was to send Garrison to England to linkup with important abolitionist leaders in that country thus making him an even more important movement leader in the United States. The NEASS was the first of the abolitionist groups that would become know later collectively as Garrisonians.[56]

The next year Garrison helped establish the American Anti-Slavery Society (AASS) that grew in a matter of just a few years into an organization with chapters spread across the northern United States. Garrison is generally credited with single-handedly drafting the AASS' Declaration of Sentiments which not only opposed slavery but also racism, colonization and violence of any kind thus dictating the group's early efforts and direction.[57] Garrison again made sure that the AASS founding Declaration stated that slavery "required its immediate abandonment, without expatriation."[58] As with the NEASS his influence would be more of a philosophical nature and less in an operational position with other notable movement leaders like Arthur and Lewis Tappan, Elizur Wright, and William Green vying for functional control of the leadership positions. His control in the AASS would be less absolute than the NEASS but it still added to his growing influence.[59] These organizations, along with his newspaper, served as his power base to circulate the Garrisonian ideology. Garrison was then ready to pursue in resolute manner his ideological objectives.

8 IDEALOGICAL BATTLES

Above and beyond his tangible battles with the pro-slavery South and sympathetic racist groups that raised mobs against abolitionists in the North, Garrison waged a kind of ideological war over his personal ideas and beliefs. His first objective as a national abolitionist leader was to take on the very popular anti-slavery ACS by publishing a pamphlet titled *Thoughts on African Colonization* in 1832. The pamphlet denounced the ACS as working hand in hand with evil slave owners to delay serious emancipation in the present by advocating the impractical repatriation of Blacks to Africa in the far flung future.[60]

The ACS was popular with the general population that just

wanted the Black slave problem to go away and conventional politicians who wanted to avoid or delay any difficult decisions. The ACS's actions included a small elite membership working exclusively through legislative action and the court system. The ACS successes tended to be limited to helping individual slaves win freedom in court, inconsequential legislation and a general sense that something was being done.[61] As an ACS supporter Garrison eventually came to see that participating completely in the political process had ultimately resulted in the ACS compromising its fundamental goal to end slavery.[62]

As a former gradualist Garrison's transition to the immediate end of slavery was complete and one only has to read his thoughts on the subject to understand his position. For example, Garrison's disdain and contempt for the ACS' racist policy of deportation of African Americans occurred over thirty-five times in the first volume of his letters alone.[63] In one letter, Garrison bluntly describes ACS members' condescension for blacks,

> . . . in a single sentence: *they have an antipathy against the blacks*. They do not wish to admit them to an

equality. They can tolerate them only as servants and slaves . . . . They tell us that we must always be hostile to the people of color, while they remain in this country. If this be so, then we had better burn our bibles, and our Declaration of Independence . . .[64]

In the *Liberator* he quoted an ACS member as saying that teaching Blacks to read was bad and would only encourage them to stay in the United States to which Garrison said, "Here is the cloven foot of colonization."[65] This personal battle against the ACS would be one that Garrison would fight relentlessly for the next thirty years. In the end he was successful along with other supportive anti-ACS advocates in rendering the once powerful organization to virtual obscurity. The battle with the ACS was amalgamating to both Garrison's followers and to the Immediate Abolitionist movement as a whole. Not all of Garrison's ideas would have this binding effect on the immediate abolitionist membership.

Other causes and ideas would develop as Garrison refined his ideology and expanded his view of the world. An important example of his maturing philosophy was his outlook on religion. As a young boy he was raised in his mother's orthodox religion and seemed to embrace the Baptist faith well into adulthood. But as he moved beyond his simple upbringing Garrison was exposed to new ideas. One such novel religious concept was Garrison's contact with the Perfectionism belief when he met with Perfectionist leader John Noyes in 1837.[66] The basic idea of Perfectionism was that through individual freewill one could live a life without sin. Garrison adopted this belief but for many of his fellow abolitionists the Perfectionist religion was too radical, rejected the old religious hierarchical control of an individual's religious life, and was ultimately a serious distraction to the abolitionist cause.

This charge of divisiveness by the more orthodox abolitionists would be leveled more than once against the idealistic Garrison. For Garrison however Perfectionism was logical and fit with his anti-slavery ideology in that man singularly and collectively could reject the sin of slavery.[67] Perfectionism would lead Garrison to see slavery not as a single social issue but a systemic problem with both a sinful state and the church tied to the institution of slavery.

Another group that had problems with Garrison was the clergy of the mainstream faiths. By 1837 there was war outside and inside the movement between Garrison and the powerful religious hierarchy in the North. This was the group he called, "a cage of unclean birds, and synagogue of Satan."[68] At the center of the debate was Garrison's anti-Sabbath belief which he used to attack what he believed was a pro-slavery clergy both in the North and the South.

He alleged that the Sabbath rather than being the one holy day of the week was just another day. In fact, everyday was just as holy as the Sabbath and people should not practice their faith only on Sunday. In a public letter Garrison said, "The Christian Sabbath is not one of time; it is not dependent upon recurrence of one day in seven; it sanctifies every moment, and, being wholly spiritual, comes not by observation."[69] What the Sabbath had become to Garrison was a way for a corrupt clergy to control the population which had lost the real meaning of religion. By taking this position on the Sabbath he felt he was logically combating the elements in society that were helping to preserve the institution of slavery.

Garrison's growing radical beliefs served to further fracture the AASS unity with leaders like Lewis Tappan saying he was taking positions, "that had better not have been discussed."[70] The attacks by pro-clergy elements like James Birney and Henry Stanton would grow so strong that Garrison would write in the *Liberator* of a diabolical clerical plot out to get him removed from the abolitionist movement.[71] In fact, Amos A. Phelps with others would found a parallel NEAA pro-clergy organization called the Massachusetts Abolition Society in 1839.[72] Undeterred, Garrison went on to flesh out his personal beliefs and by natural extension of his position and influence the movement's doctrine.

A less conflictive position, at least in the beginning of the movement, was Garrison's nonresistance stance. Garrison had been a pacifist most of his adult life and had even avoided militia training as a young man.[73] In 1838 Garrison, as with other organizations he belonged to, even wrote the Declaration of

Sentiments for the Non-Resistance Society at their founding convention in Boston.[74] When Lovejoy was killed a year earlier Garrison had praised his abolitionist position but still found fault in the futility of his taking up arms. Garrison wrote in the *Liberator*, "They were not required as philanthropists or Christians; and they have certainly set a dangerous precedent in the maintenance of our cause."[75] Naturally his feelings on violence and slavery combined with his overall ideology.

The nonresistance position Garrison believed and advocated would vex him over the years. Still, he always held that nonviolence was the personal answer for him and felt that it was also best for the movement. Still, when he wrote of the bellicose nature of Walker's *Appeal* in the *Liberator* Garrison said, "If any people were ever justified in throwing off the yoke of their tyrants, the slaves are that people."[76] Even when his son George joined the Union Army in 1863 Garrison tried to appeal to his principles of peace. But in the end Garrison did not reject his soldier son and expressed his concerns for him as would any good father.[77] Garrison was a man who idealized peace but he empathized with others' need to stand up and fight the evil of slavery.[78]

Perhaps his most fundamental idea about combating slavery was that of moral suasion. Moral suasion would come to permeate his strategies and further radicalize the message. The concept was that the end of slavery required people to change their not their laws, public institutions, politics, or government but the way they thought in a fundamental way.[79] To stop slavery one had to not just make it illegal but make association in any form with the institution of slavery immoral throughout the entire North. Once the Southern people saw divine righteousness in the North they would naturally follow suit and end slavery forever.[80] In some ways moral suasion was a logical extension of his Perfectionist beliefs, nonresistance stand, the political failures of the ACS and his own petition drives, and the overall rejection of mainstream religious denominations to confront the sin of slavery. Garrison's idea of moral suasion would prove to be the key concept that ultimately divided the Immediate Abolitionist movement between those that wanted to work within the system and those that wanted to go directly to the people to cause change.

However the spark that actually fractured the movement was the Garrisonian idea on women's rights in the Antebellum United States. From the beginning the movement had been keen to attract women. Garrison enthusiastically supported women-led populist petition drives that overwhelmed the United States Congress by their sheer volume.[81] He was also supportive of other women-led efforts like abolitionist fairs which raised huge amounts of money.[82] More importantly, he encouraged women to participate not in auxiliary organizations but in the main abolitionist societies in key leadership roles and even to participate in 'Promiscuous' audiences with both men and women in attendance.[83] In an 1839 open letter Garrison affirmed that the NEAS constitution (which he wrote) stated, "That we consider the anti-slavery cause of philanthropy, with regard to all human beings ... MEN and WOMEN, have the same duties and same rights."[84] Women such as Sarah and Angelina Grimke, and Maria Chapman within the movement became an important power base for Garrison to use and protect.[85] His public discussion on the need for women's rights was primary reserved for the pages of the *Liberator*. But it was difficult to dissociate Garrison the publisher, and Garrison the abolitionist leader, so naturally the debate flowed over into society meetings.[86] His inclusion of women further provoked more conservative society members already upset at Garrison's other radical ideas. Garrison, in an 1839 letter, cites some of the agitators, "Phelps, St. Clair, Torrey, Wise, &c., I learned intend to organize a new and hostile society next week, which will put down the women, the Childs, the Chapmans, the Grimkes, and the Kellys from active participation in anti-slavery meeting ... "[87] This fight of women in the movement would come to a head in 1838-1840 and set off a series of organizational fractures over Garrison's principal ideology.

The concepts just discussed were the core ideas that evolved and defined Garrison ideology and his life during the 1820s and 1830s. There were others ideas which shaped Garrison's thinking but these beliefs provided the structure for him as a man and abolitionist leader. They also defined Garrison's responses to the significant events that occurred such as the establishment of the *Liberator*, incorporation of a respectable middle class life style, his philosophical involvement in the genesis of the immediate abolition movement in the United States, and his ideological battles with Southerners, mainstream clergy, anti-Black and pro-slavery Northerners and the ACS. This period would be the intellectual pinnacle in his ideological development that stimulated the growth of the Immediate Abolitionist movement. From this point on Garrison's reputation would continue to grow but his influence on the movement would become more isolated. At the same time, Garrison's advancement of his professional philosophy would seem at first look decidedly more radical in nature. The chaotic times of the 1840s and 1850s eventually would become a period of ups and downs in Garrison's role as an abolitionist leader.

It should be noted that his private life was more in line with his vision as a stable family man. From his happy marriage in 1834 to his wife Helen, Garrison would fill his correspondence with such expressions as found in an 1876 letter,

> For was there ever a more loving wife, or a more affectionate and devoted mother? How strong was the magnetism with which held us together! And such a home as made for me for more than two score years! And how blessed she made it for all her children![88]

He and Helen would have five boys and one girl of which all but one would outlive their parents.[89] As a family they seemed very devoted to one another and without major strife. Garrison was a loving father who enjoying being around his wife and children. Even after his children were grown there was a great deal of positive interaction. Garrison said in an 1875 letter to Wendell Phillips, "I have more satisfaction and comfort in my children than words can express."[90] He also was supportive of his extended family caring for his wife's elderly parents in their last years, and his brother James who came to live with him until he died of cancer.[91] Garrison lived up to his ideal of a loving and caring father who could always be counted on. His family in turn would provide him solace during the difficult period building up to the Civil War.

9 GARRISONIANS AND NON-GARRISONIANS

The 1830s had been a period of growth in the Immediate Abolitionist movement with hundreds of societies forming a mass movement in the Northern states.[92] Garrison and his ideology had ridden the crest of that populist wave. However, by the end of the decade the movement suffered the fate of most social movements and had matured and grown to incorporate various interest groups such as Evangelists, Nonresistants, Transcendentalists, Quakers, and Political-Action Abolitionists.[93] There had been other groups earlier on but Garrison and his related societies had been the innovative leaders in large part because of the aforementioned ideas. As the movement began to fracture Garrison was normally to be found at the center or at least had a very public position on the disagreement. In time, historians would come to title these different interest groups within the movement as either Garrisonians or Non-Garrisonians and Anti-Garrisonians.[94] The disagreements in the late 1830s over the Garrisonian position on the Sabbath and women's roles were building to a showdown within the movement which finally occurred at the beginning of the 1840s.

The internal conflict reached a high point in the AASS during 1840 between the political-action Anti-Garrisonians and the moralist Garrisonians. Garrison and his followers prophetically believed that any political third party based on the single issue of slavery would ultimately fail and in the end those in the party would compromise their morality as the ACS had earlier.[95] Garrison, while a nonvoter himself, believed abolitionists had more power lobbying the political major parties while remaining morally distant from corrupt politicians. He said at one point, "use all parties and sects . . . but be used by none."[96] This was a position he maintained as long as the Union consisted of both a North and pro-slave South, and during the glory days of the Liberty Party and to a lesser degree the Free Soil Party.

Garrison won the ideological battle within the society and with his 600 followers retained philosophical control of the AASS. However, he would lose the ideological war for control of the mass movement to the losers like the Tappan brothers, James Birney and Henry Stanton who marched off to form the more popular Liberty Party. [97] The same year Garrison would make the second of his five trips to England and would become embroiled in more controversy. His ideas on women's rights would result in his detaching himself from the London-based World Anti-Slavery Conference in order to sit with the excluded female AASS members in the balcony.[98] In both cases Garrison followed his beliefs and in both cases he diminished his overall influence within the mass movement.

The 1840s would also usher in the refinement of Garrison's moral suasion notion in a more radical form. He would finally and completely embrace the idea of the disunion of the United States which would brand him a true radical. Garrison said explicitly in an 1842 letter, "I am for the repeal of the union between the North and South - alias between LIBERTY and SLAVERY."[99] Until the onset of the Civil War, he decried the Constitution as a proslavery document and advocated the breakup of the Union as the only answer to the slavery question. His letters continue to reflect his thoughts on other basic beliefs such as his position about the role the Constitution played in the institution of slavery, "I pronounce it the most bloody and heaven-daring arrangement ever made by men for the continuance and protection of a system of the most atrocious villainy ever exhibited on earth."[100] In another letter he even refers to the Constitution as the "covenant with death."[101] He makes similar censorious remarks about the Constitution with growing regularity no less than thirty times between 1833 and 1858.[102] During a speech Garrison even burned a copy of the Constitution at a 4th of July abolitionist picnic in 1854 while saying, "So perish all compromises with tyranny and let all the people say, Amen."[103] This idea that slavery could only end by a dissolution of the United States into a separate North and South would be Garrison's signature idea during the buildup to the war.

Garrison also traveled more than ever before on the lecture circuit along with Wendell Phillips, Frederick Douglass and others over the next two decades. He became a popular speaker and publicly well known across the nation speaking on a variety of topics such as the evils of the Mexican War, the need for social reform, women's rights, nonviolence, the moral corruption of the church and state, the need for disunion and most importantly the ultimate end of the number one sin of slavery. This public recognition however did not make the infamous Garrison and his ideas less radical.[104] He continued to press the aforementioned ideas in ever stronger terms during speeches and in the *Liberator*.[105] Significantly the national press also acted as his forum repeating his titillating and outlandish pronouncements in their papers across the country.[106]

However, by the 1850s Garrison's message was diminished by the violence in the aftermath of the Kansas-Nebraska Act of 1854. Garrison's nonviolent message was pushed to the side in a nation seemingly bent on a violent civil war.[107] During this time the AASS and NEAS drastically lost membership as former Garrisonians shifted to political movements like the Republican Party.[108] At the same time, his radical message of disunion seemed less and less drastic as others like John Brown preached a violent revolt.[109] Nevertheless, Garrison stayed on message always pushing his nonresistance form of moral suasion as before. He also remained in the public eye as one of the best known abolitionists of the Antebellum period. In the 1859 edition of *The New American Cyclopaedia: A Popular Dictionary of General Knowledge* Garrison rated more space than, "Emerson, Thoreau, Stowe, Phillips, and Douglass combined."[110] With events like the Dred Scott case happening in the latter 1850's, many in the North were less skeptical about Garrison's and other abolitionists' accusations against slavery. Even conventional politicians were campaigning against the status quo such as when Lincoln in 1858 said "I believe this government cannot endure, permanently half *slave* and half *free*".[111] the union could not go on "half-slave, half-free." Garrison commented that some members of the main stream press "now . . . treat abolitionists with respect . . . and refer to their doctrines and measures without misrepresentation."[112] The 1850s proved a period of very undulating fortunes for Garrison and his professional standing.

10 POPULAR PROPHET AND REPUBLICAN ADVOCATE

The beginning of the war would cause an even greater sea change for Garrison's reputation but not in his personal opinions and ideas. For example, Garrison was totally uncompromising in his opinions about fellow abolitionists' thoughts, beliefs and positions. When speaking of his former ally Frederick Douglass in 1860, he was unrestrained, "I regard him as thoroughly base and selfish, and I know that his hostility to the American Anti-Slavery Society . . . is unmitigated and unceasing."[113] Even his close friend, Wendell Phillips, was not protected from Garrison's criticism when they disagreed on support for President Lincoln, "While he [Wendell Phillips] is still listened to for his oratorical ability, his criticisms are daily becoming less valuable and less regarded."[114] As can be seen from his letters, Garrison was more than willing to express himself on other abolitionist's viewpoints when they disagreed with him or his ideology. The times and people had changed but not Garrison's fundamental beliefs, ideology and sense of self-righteous in any situation.

At the same time, Garrison became a mainstream commentator and Republican supporter during the Civil War. He still believed that slavery was a sin but his radical call for disunion had in fact come to pass. Not the way he foresaw or hoped it would unfold in a nonviolent conversion of the society but nonetheless it was happening.[115] The Civil War had in essence broken the 'Covenant with Death' and restored the Constitution.[116] He was even willing to curb his nonviolent stance in the face of this juggernaut of a war, "Let us all stand aside when the North is rushing like a tornado in the right direction."[117] Nevertheless, Garrison was not uncritical when he saw the Republicans and Lincoln doing something that violated his ideology as shown by one 1861 letter which referred to the President's limited mental powers, "If he is 6 feet 4 inches high, he is only a dwarf in mind."[118] Any perceived equivocation by Lincoln on the issue of ending slavery would quickly draw Garrison's public angst while continuing to support the general war effort.[119] After Lincoln signed the 1863 Emancipation Proclamation Garrison's words were normally filled admiration rather than scorn for Lincoln and his party. By the end of the war Garrison was completely in Lincoln's camp writing personal words of praise to the President and with a sense of familiarity recommending a friend for a cabinet position.[120]

In popular culture he had at last become the respected senior statesman for the Immediate Abolitionist movement and a prophet who seen the end of slavery and to some extent the conflict that had ensued.[121] With the ratification of the Thirteenth Amendment in 1865 the sixty year old Garrison publicly concluded that he and the abolitionist movement's mission to end slavery was complete. He ended publication of the *Liberator* after thirty plus years and prepared for retirement. He even attempted to close the abolitionist societies which were closely associated with him. Others in the movement, to include his old associate Phillips, would publicly opposed his efforts.[122] As a result, the AASS and NEAS would continue for a few short years under Phillips' control but without Garrison's vision they also closed shop for good. [123] Garrison's professional career as a fulltime abolition idealist was at last over.

11 POST WAR RETIREMENT

Many would accuse Garrison of ending his fulltime participation in abolitionism not because of his ideology but because of his ego and the need for public praise. In truth, Garrison did feel that veneration was justified for all his work over the years but he also believed that the abolitionist mission was actually accomplished. He had for over thirty years unwaveringly followed his ideology when an entire nation seemed against it. He had seen his foremost idea, that slavery was inherently evil and therefore must end, actually come to pass. There were other social causes and advocacy groups but he felt that with the abolition of slavery in the United States there was just no practical need for societies with abolition in the title.[124] In Garrison's mind this seemed to rightly be a time of reflection on the successes of his ideology and rewards that derived from it which would include two triumphant trips overseas, to Europe in 1867 and England 1877.[125]

In the end he was a man well content with himself and secure in a retirement funded by his friends and many admirers. As reflected in his letters to family members Garrison found a great deal of happiness in the simple pleasures of home, family and caring for his wife who had suffered a debilitating stroke in 1863.[126] His letters also indicate that Garrison continued to generate a large amount of public and private correspondence for various social causes such as women's rights, the freedmen cause, Chinese immigration, pacifism, and temperance.[127] He even reconciled with some of his colleagues in the abolitionist movement who had dared to disagree with his philosophy including Phillips who as a gesture of friendship would preside at Helen's funeral.[128] His controversial time as a full time philosopher, social advocate, newspaper editor and nonviolent provocateur were at an end. William Lloyd Garrison passed away a year after Helen's death at home among family on May 24, 1879.[129]

12 HISTORIOGRAPHICAL REVIEW

The controversy surrounding Garrison did not end with his death, rather it moved into the scholarly field of historical studies. The following provides a brief historiographical analysis of the changing interpretations of Garrison and his ideology. Since becoming a historical figure Garrison's reputation has ebbed and flowed through various renditions. There are almost as many versions of William L. Garrison as there are historians writing about him. The reason for this is in large part due to the nature of his professional career. As discussed earlier Garrison's life revolved around his ideology. Therefore, most of the analysis of

Garrison also revolves around ideology and its influence which leaves a great deal of room for interpretation and conjecture. The following is a representative selection of the books and articles from 1873 to the present focusing almost exclusively on Garrison.

The interpretations from the late 1800s best examined are Henry Wilson's *History of the Rise and Fall of the Slave Power in America* and James Rhodes' *History of the United States from the Compromise of 1850 Volume I 1850-1854*.[130] Importantly, both writers experienced the Civil War, had a contemporary understanding of the period and provide a unique perspective compared to later writers in the field. They also portray two different versions of Garrison and the degree of his influence on abolitionist movement and the general population of the North.

Beginning with Wilson's explanation of Garrison's life the reader is presented with an idealistic but radical Garrison whose influence was limited. In one chapter of his 1877 book Wilson talked about how the abolition movement was really an outgrowth of the Christian religion.[131] The radical Garrison and the Garrisonians, "never constituted more than a fraction of the antislavery host. The veteran William Goodell estimated their number at about one eighth. The large majority of Abolitionists retained their connection with both the ecclesiastical and political organizations of the land."[132]

Rhodes' later 1892 book presented a less radical and more influential Garrison. He said, "The apostle who had especial fitness for the work, and who now came forward to embody this feeling and rouse the national conscience from the stupor of great material prosperity, was Garrison."[133] He goes on in another chapter to explain that Garrison's influence went well beyond his followers and included, "never-ceasing inculcation on those who were already voters and on thinking youths who were to become voters, and who, in their turn, prevailed upon others."[134] Rhodes even went so far as to say that Garrison helped establish the Republican Party, "Yet the only practical result of their labor lay in the fact that, having convinced men that slavery was wrong, they made Republican voters, while they were urging their followers not vote."[135]

The next century's study of Garrison kicked off with a 1913 Garrison biography by another radical, John Jay Chapman. His essay praising Garrison for being a radical was considered too radical itself and was disregarded by historians of the time.[136] Today his biography has achieved more respect, "John Jay Chapman, William Lloyd Garrison (N.Y., 1913), is a biographical essay of great discernment."[137] It was not until 1933 with Gilbert Barnes' *The Antislavery Impulse* that Garrison's historiography made major progress in the study of abolitionism and Garrison. An example of its influence can be found in the books and articles that have cited *The Antislavery Impulse* since its publication.[138] Barnes paints a less than flattering picture of Garrison. He depicts him as a totally self-centered fanatic, hated by those in the movement except for his closest followers but who, for whatever reason, became the personification of the movement.[139] In Barnes words,

> The time had passed . . . when he could be cashiered or voluntarily leave the ranks . . . . Though the

Massachusetts society split apart and the movement in New England fell into hopeless disrepute, Garrison still remained a hero to his disciples and the legendary figure of abolitionism to the nation.[140]

The remaining 1930s and 1940s was a time when Garrison and abolitionists in general were simply disregarded at best as madmen or at worst a contributing factor to a needless war.[141] The 1950s would be the next period of reassessment of Garrison and his ideology.

Russel Nye's biography titled *William Lloyd Garrison and the Humanitarian Reformers* in 1955 was the first book length work on Garrison. It was overall a favorable interpretation of Garrison. He presented Garrison as not a god or a demon but a man with strengths and weaknesses. Nye's Garrison was an important abolitionist but not the underpinning to the movement, "The movement, set in motion by others, was carried to its conclusion by methods he could not accept and ideas he could not understand. Abolition passed through him, not from him."[142] The Civil Rights movement in the 1960s provided a new point of reference and additional relevancy for further study of abolitionists and Garrison.[143]

The book that best reflected Garrison's resurgence in the 1960s was Aileen Kraditor's *Means and Ends in American Abolitionism*.[144] In her biography she reformed Garrison into a pragmatic thinker and even gave him a sense of humor.[145] She also made him the spiritual leader and the center of philosophical debate in the movement.[146] The main argument was that it was not Garrison and his followers who had unrealistic goals for the abolitionist movement, rather abolitionists who wanted to turn the movement into a political party were the ones that were unrealistic.[147] With this work Garrison returned to an important level of influence and standing within the abolitionist movement and the general culture around the time of the Civil War.

Since the 1970s there have been a large number of books and articles on the abolitionist movement. They have explored different social aspects to include women, minorities in the North, racism, religion, economic change, and republicanism in order to understand Northern culture and the movement itself.[148] The books reviewed for this work which were written between 1970 to present have Garrison figuring prominently as a leader and major participant in the Immediate Abolitionist movement. During this period another major contribution to the study of Garrison was the multi volume set of Garrison letters produced by Walter M. Merrill and Louis Ruchames between 1971 and 1981. In 1994 there was also a collection of articles from the *Liberator* edited by William Cain. One of the latest major Garrison biographies titled *All On Fire: William Lloyd Garrison and the Abolition of Slavery* continued the premise of Garrison as a key figure in the abolitionist movement. The author promotes Garrison as no less than "an authentic American hero who, with a biblical prophet's power and a propagandist's skill, forced the nation to confront the most crucial moral issue in its history."[149] If this 1998 book is any indication Garrison's resurgence has not abated.

13 CONCLUSION

It is fitting that Garrison's life is seen against the backdrop of his ideas rather than using the events that occurred during his time on earth as a yardstick. As seen, Garrison himself was very much controlled by his ideas and filtered his actions through his ideology. He was in some ways very German in following his inner voice just like Martin Luther when he spoke at the Diet of Worms, "I cannot and I will not retract anything, since it is neither safe nor right to go against conscience."[150] As a young man Garrison seemed to draw strength from his internal ideas and sense of self. He invented himself around his inner ideology and continued to follow his ideas even when threatened by mob violence.

Garrison's life revolved around his ideology and expounding his ideas to the public opened him up to scrutiny by everyone. Since at the time his ideas were considered radical and revolutionary the man and the ideas were the subjects of wide-ranging judgments. Garrison's ideology was rather simple and easy to understand for those that got past the rhetoric of the age. His message called for the nonviolent end to slavery, equality for men and women, a church and government free of corruption and the fair treatment of all. True, Garrison's vision was an idealistic view of the world but it was a vision he held true to his entire life.

Studying Garrison it is almost impossible to separate the man from his philosophy. A close study of both his private and public letters produces an image of a man devoted to his family and his personal beliefs. In fact, most of his letters to family and friends blended his private thoughts with his professional beliefs on social reform. He seemed to seldom stray far from the internalized vision of Garrison the abolitionist leader, editor and social commentator. Even when courting his wife Garrison found room in his love letters to talk about ending slavery.

As a historical figure Garrison is noteworthy in the function he performed in relationship to the abolitionist movement. He and his ideology did produce a small group of abolition followers and a modest readership for the *Liberator*. More importantly, his public position on issues like slavery, the Constitution, the Sabbath, nonviolence, and women's rights produced a great deal of debate which seemed to help keep the issue of immediate emancipation in the public eye throughout the Antebellum and Civil War period. It was his dogged adherence and the controversy of his ideas that in the end gave them staying power.

A brief review the historiography of Garrison has also shown the controversy and longevity of his ideas. Since he did not lead a great army of followers, control vast amounts of political patronage or rule a huge publishing empire his affect on the movement to end slavery has been hard to gauge. Garrison's primary currency was the fathomless ideology he advocated in his letters, speeches, and newspaper. As a result, Garrison and his ideology have and will continue to produce much debate as to their meaning, origin and affect.

SELECTED BIBLIOGRAPHY

Barnes, Gilbert Hobbs. <u>The Antislavery Impulse 1830-1844</u>. n.p.: The American Historical Association, 1933; reprint, Gloucester, Mass.: Peter Smith, 1957.

Cain, William E. <u>William Lloyd Garrison and the Fight Against Slavery : Selections from The Liberator</u>. Boston Bedford/St. Martin's, 1994.

Dillon, Merton L. "The Abolitionists: A Decade of Historiography, 1959-1969." <u>The Journal of Southern History</u> 35, (Nov 1969): 500-522.

Fredrickson, George M. ed. <u>William Lloyd Garrison</u>. Englewood Cliffs: Prentice Hall, Inc., 1968.

Friedman, Lawrence J. "Abolitionists versus Historians." <u>Reviews in American History</u> 5, (Sep 1977): 342-347.

Goodman, Paul. <u>Of One Blood: Abolitionism and the Origins of Racial Equality</u>. Berkeley: University of California Press, 1998.

Huston, James L. "The Experimental Basis of Northern Antislavery Impulse," <u>The Journal of Southern History</u> 56, (Nov 1990): 609.

Jacobs, Donald M., ed. <u>Courage and Conscience: Black & White Abolitionists in Boston</u> Bloomington: Indiana University Press, 1993.

Kraditor, Aileen S. <u>Means and Ends in American Abolitionism: Garrison and His Critics on Strategy and Tactics, 1834-1850</u>. n.p.: Pantheon Books, 1969; reprinted, Chicago: Elephant Paperback, 1989.

Lindberg, Carter. <u>The European Reformations</u>. Malden, Mass: Blackwell

Publishers Inc., 2001.

May, Henry. All On Fire: William Lloyd Garrison and the Abolition of Slavery. New York: St. Martin's Press, 1998.

Mayer, Henry. "William Lloyd Garrison: The Undisputed Master of the Cause of Negro Liberation." The Journal of Blacks in Higher Education no. 23 (Spring 1999): 105-109.

Merrill, Walter M., Against Wind And Tide: A Biography of Wm. Lloyd Garrison. Cambridge, Mass.: Harvard University Press, 1963.

_____, ed. The Letters of William Lloyd Garrison Volume I: I Will Be Heard! 1822-1835. Cambridge: The Belknap Press of Harvard University Press, 1971.

_____, ed. The Letters of William Lloyd Garrison Volume III: No Union With Slave-holders 1841-1849. Cambridge: The Belknap Press of Harvard University Press, 1973.

_____, ed. The Letters of William Lloyd Garrison Volume V: Let the Oppressed Go Free 1861-1867: Let the Oppressed Go Free. Cambridge: The Belknap Press of Harvard University Press, 1979.

Merrill, Walter M., and Louis Ruchames, eds. The Letters of William Lloyd Garrison Volume VI: To Rouse the Slumbering Land 1868-1879. Cambridge: The Belknap Press of Harvard University Press, 1981.

Nye, Russel B. William Lloyd Garrison and the Humanitarian Reformers. ed. Oscar Handlin. Boston and Toronto: Little, Brown and Company, 1955.

Portner, Stuart. "The Abolition Movement." The Mississippi Valley Historical Review 24, (Sep 1937): 218-220.

Rhodes, James Ford. History of the United States from the Compromise of 1850 Volume I 1850-1854. n.p., 1892; reprinted, New York: The

Macmillan Company, 1900.

_____. History of the United States from the Compromise of 1850 Volume II 1854-1860. n.p., 1892; reprinted, New York: The Macmillan Company, 1900.

Rohrback, Augusta. "Truth Stronger and Stranger Than Fiction: Reexamining William Lloyd Garrison's *Liberator*." American Literature 73, (Dec 2001): 727-755.

Ruchames, Louis. "William Lloyd Garrison and the Negro Franchise." The Journal of Negro History 50, (Jan 1965): 37-49.

_____, ed. The Letters of William Lloyd Garrison Volume II: A House Dividing Against Itself 1836-1840. Cambridge: The Belknap Press of Harvard University Press, 1971.

_____, ed. The Letters of William Lloyd Garrison Volume IV: From Disunionism to the Brink of War 1850-1860. Cambridge: The Belknap Press of Harvard University Press, 1975.

Stewart, James B. Holy Warriors: The Abolitionists and American Slavery. New York: Hill and Wang, 1996.

Strong, Douglas M. Perfectionist Politics: Abolitionism and the Religious Tensions of American Democracy. New York: Syracuse University Press, 1999.

Thomas, John L. The Liberator: William Lloyd Garrison. Boston: Little, Brown and Company, 1963.

Walters, Ronald G. The Antislavery Appeal: American Abolitionism after 1830. New York: W. W. W. Norton and Company, 1984.

Wilson, Henry. History of the Rise and Fall of the Slave Power in America Volume III. Boston: James R. Osgood and Company, 1877; reprint, New York: Negro Universities Press, 1969.

Yellin, Jean Fagan and John C. Van Horne, eds. <u>The Abolitionist Sisterhood: Women's Political Cultural in Antebellum America</u>. Ithaca and London: Cornell University Press, 1994.

ABOUT THE AUTHOR

Tim Pifer is a retired Army Lieutenant Colonel living in Louisville, Kentucky. He has a Bachelors of Science Degree in Criminal Justice from West Virginia State College, a Master of Arts Degree in Education from National-Louis University, Master of Arts Degree in History from the University of Louisville, and Master of Science in Library and Information Science from Drexel University.

ENDNOTES

[1] Aileen S. Kraditor, *Means and Ends in American Abolitionism* (Chicago: Ivan R. Dee, Inc., 1989), 12.

[2] Walter M. Merrill and Louis Ruchames, eds., *The Letters of William Lloyd Garrison, Volumes 1-6,* (Cambridge, The Belknap Press of Harvard University Press, 1971-1981).

[3] Walter M. Merrill, ed., *The Letters of William Lloyd Garrison Volume I 1822-1835* (Cambridge, The Belknap Press of Harvard University Press, 1971), vii-xxv.

[4] Ibid., 5-6.

[5] Louis Ruchames, ed., *The Letters of William Lloyd Garrison Volume IV 1850-1860* (Cambridge, The Belknap Press of Harvard University Press, 1975), 702-704.

[6] Walter M. Merrill, ed., *The Letters of William Lloyd Garrison Volume V 1861-1867* (Cambridge, The Belknap Press of Harvard University Press, 1979), xv.

[7] Walter M. Merrill, and Louis Ruchames, eds., *The Letters of William Lloyd Garrison Volume VI 1868-1879* (Cambridge, The Belknap Press of Harvard University Press, 1981), xvii.

[8] Ruchames, *Volume IV*, 421.

[9] Ibid.

[10] Walter M. Merrill, ed., *The Letters of William Lloyd Garrison Volume III 1841-1849* (Cambridge, The Belknap Press of Harvard University Press, 1973), 620.

[11] Walter M. Merrill, *Against Wind And Tide: A Biography of Wm. Lloyd Garrison* (Cambridge, Mass.: Harvard University Press, 1963), 1-2.

[12] Henry May, *All On Fire: William Lloyd Garrison and the Abolition of Slavery* (New York: St. Martin's Press, 1998), 12-13.

[13] John L. Thomas, *The Liberator: William Lloyd Garrison* (Boston: Little, Brown and Company, 1963), 18-20.

[14] May, 4-9.

[15] Thomas, 307-309.

[16] Merrill, *Volume VI*, 337.

[17] Merrill, *Volume III*, 538.

[18] Ibid., 17.

[19] May, 103-104.

[20] Walter M. Merrill, ed., *The Letters of William Lloyd Garrison Volume I 1822-1835* (Cambridge, The Belknap Press of Harvard University Press, 1971), 368-369.

[21] Merrill, *Volume III*, 354.

[22] Thomas, 20-21.

[23] Merrill, *Volume III*, 79.

[24] Ibid., 587.

[25] Merrill, *Volume V*, 539.

[26] Ibid., 118.

[27] Merrill, *Volume VI*, 388-390.

[28] Merrill, *Against Wind And Tide*, 11.

[29] Russel B. Nye, *William Lloyd Garrison and the Humanitarian Reformers*, ed. Oscar Handlin, (Boston and Toronto: Little, Brown and Company, 1955), 11.

[30] Merrill, *Volume I*, 11.

[31] May, 33.

[32] Merrill, *Volume I*, 24.

[33] Ibid., 47.

[34] Ibid.

[35] Ibid., 55-56.

[36] Ibid., 179.

[37] May, 40-43.

[38] Thomas, 67.

[39] Ibid., 54-59.

[40] Ibid., 93.

[41] Paul Goodman, *Of One Blood: Abolitionism and the Origins of Racial Equality* (Berkeley, University of California Press, 1998), 41-42

[42] Ibid., 102.

[43] Merrill, *Volume I*, 75.

[44] May, 85-93.

[45] Nye, 24-25.

[46] James B. Stewart, *Holy Warriors: The Abolitionists and American Slavery* (New York, Hill and Wang, 1996), 40-42.

[47] Kraditor, ix.

[48] Ibid., 1.

[49] May, 111.

[50] Ibid.

[51] Augusta Rohrback, "Truth Stronger and Stranger Than Fiction: Reexamining William Lloyd Garrison's *Liberator*," *American Literature* 73, (Dec 2001): 727-755.

[52] Ibid., 727.

[53] Merrill, *Volume III*, 105.

[54] Merrill, *Volume I*, 163.

[55] Nye, 57.

[56] Douglas M. Strong, *Perfectionist Politics: Abolitionism and the Religious Tensions of American Democracy* (New York: Syracuse University Press, 1999), 13.

[57] Stewart, *Holy Warriors*, 51-52.

[58] Kraditor, 5.

[59] Merrill, *Against Wind And Tide*, 79-81.

[60] Thomas, 147-154.

[61] Goodman, 11-22.

[62] Ibid., 36-37.

[63] Merrill, *Volume I*, 116, 122, 155, 173-176, 193-194, 235-236, 242, 245-246, 252-256, 260, 263-264, 268, 269, 281, 290, 299, 441, 446-447, 460-463, 517.

[64] Ibid., 124.

[65] Merrill, *Against Wind And Tide*, 63.

[66] Strong, 37.

[67] Ronald G. Walters, *The Antislavery Appeal: American Abolitionism after 1830* (New York: W. W. W. Norton and Company, 1984), 12-14.

[68] Merrill, *Against Wind And Tide*, 132.

[69] Louis Ruchames, ed., *The Letters of William Lloyd Garrison Volume II 1836-1840* (Cambridge, The Belknap Press of Harvard University Press, 1971), 148.

[70] May, 236.

[71] Kraditor, 96-97.

[72] Ibid., 100.

[73] May, 224.

[74] Ruchames, *Volume II*, 333.

[75] Thomas, 257.

[76] Donald M. Jacobs, ed. *Courage and Conscience: Black & White Abolitionists in Boston* (Bloomington: Indiana University Press, 1993), 15.

[77] Merrill, *Volume V*, 160.

[78] Merrill, *Against Wind And Tide*, 273.

[79] Strong, 40.

[80] Walters, 25.

[81] Jean Fagan Yellin, and John C. Van Horne, eds. *The Abolitionist Sisterhood: Women's Political Cultural in Antebellum America* (Ithaca and London: Cornell University Press, 1994), 12-13.

[82] Ruchames, *Volume II*, 194-195.

[83] Yellin, 285-288.

[84] Ruchames, *Volume II*, 506.

[85] Thomas, 255.

[86] Kraditor, 62.

[87] Ruchames, *Volume II*, 463.

[88] Merrill, *Volume VI*, 400.

[89] Thomas, 307.

[90] Ibid., 358.

[91] May, 269-322.

[92] Goodman, 133.

[93] Nye, 128-143.

[94] Walters, 44, Nye, 147, Yellin, 263, Ruchames, *Volume II,* 553.

[95] Walters, 13-18.

[96] Nye, 149.

[97] Jacobs, 36-37.

[98] Yellin, 305-306.

[99] Merrill, *Volume III*, 57.

[100] Merrill, *Volume I*, 249.

[101] Merrill, *Volume III*, 449

[102] Merrill and Ruchames, I: 249-252, 332, 498, 521-524, II: 287, 325, 474-475, 512, III: 178, 245, 292, 293, 301, 303, 449, 516, 523, IV: 241, 381, 406, 408-409, 455, 509, 517, 569-571.

[103] May, 445.

[104] Thomas, 309-314.

[105] Ibid., 331-337.

[106] Ibid., 358-359.

[107] May, 445.

[108] Nye 163.

[109] Ibid., 166.

[110] May, 458.

[111] Stephen B. Oates, *With Malice Toward None: A Life Of Abraham Lincoln* (New York: HarperPerennial, 1994), 143.

[112] Ibid., 159.

[113] Ruchames, *Volume IV,* 693.

[114] Merrill, *Volume V*, 389.

[115] Kraditor, 216-217.

[116] Merrill, *Volume V*, 3-4.

[117] Ibid., 3.

[118] Ibid., 37.

[119] Nye, 172-173.

[120] Ibid., 255-259.

[121] Nye, 177-178.

[122] May, 569-570.

[123] Stewart 195.

[124] May, 587-591.

[125] Thomas, 445-446, 451.

[126] Merrill, *Volume VI,* 29-30, 62, 70-71, 78, 85-86, 88-90, 91-92, 101, 105-106, 108-109, 126, 128-130, 137-138, 141-143, 151, 162-163, 164-166, 167, 176, 187, 196-200-202, 203-205, 215-218, 243-244, 250, 282, 291-292, 303, 331-332, 334-336, 341-343, 357-358, 359, 375-379, 383-384, 393, 397, 398, 416-417, 444-445, 447-448, 449-450, 451-453, 467-468, 469-474, 488, 504-506, 532, 543-544, 545-548, 556-560, 562, 563-564.

[127] Ibid., 97, 106, 233-235, 263-264, 268-270, 313-314, 358, 410411, 478-480, 511-512, 524-526, 527-528, 538-539, 542, 563, 565-566, 572-573, 583-584, 585-586.

[128] Thomas, 450-451.

[129] Merrill, *Against Wind And Tide*, 330.

[130] George M. Fredrickson, ed. *William Lloyd Garrison* (Englewood Cliffs: Prentice Hall, Inc., 1968), 119, 132.

[131] Henry Wilson, *History of the Rise and Fall of the Slave Power in America*

Volume III (Boston: James R. Osgood and Company, 1877; reprint, New York: Negro Universities Press, 1969), 696-724.

[132] Ibid., 718.

[133] James Ford Rhodes, *History of the United States from the Compromise of 1850 Volume I 1850-1854* (n.p., 1892; reprinted, New York: The Macmillan Company, 1900), 55.

[134] Ibid., 62.

[135] James Ford Rhodes, *History of the United States from the Compromise of 1850 Volume II 1850-1854* (n.p., 1892; reprinted, New York: The Macmillan Company, 1900), 435.

[136] Fredrickson, 138.

[137] May, 635.

[138] Merrill, 342, Kraditor, 282, Nye, 209, Thomas, 488, Strong, 238, Goodman, x, Walters, 187, Stewart, 212 Fredrickson, 145.

[139] Gilbert Hobbs Barnes, *The Antislavery Impulse 1830-1844* (n.p.: The American Historical Association, 1933; reprint, Gloucester, Mass.: Peter Smith, 1957), 88-99.

[140] Ibid., 99.

[141] Merton L. Dillon, "The Abolitionists: A Decade of Historiography, 1959-1969." *The Journal of Southern History* 35, (Nov 1969) 500.

[142] Nye, 205.

[143] Dillon, 502.

[144] Ibid., 512.

[145] Kraditor, ix-x.

[146] Ibid., 7-10.

[147] Ibid., 165-166.

[148] James L. Huston, "The Experimental Basis of Northern Antislavery Impulse," *The Journal of Southern History* 56, (Nov 1990), 609.

[149] May, xiii.

[150] Carter Lindberg, *The European Reformations* (Malden Mass, Blackwell Publishers Inc., 2001), 89.

Timothy Pifer

THE PHILOSOPHER ABOLITIONIST

Made in the USA
Middletown, DE
07 September 2021